HERE
AND NOT
ELSEWHERE

Selected Poems: 1990-2010

ESSENTIAL TRANSLATIONS SERIES 7

[loːrən]
Übersetzerhaus Looren Collège de traducteurs Looren
Translation House Looren

swiss arts council
prᴐhelvetia

Pietro De Marchi

HERE AND NOT ELSEWHERE

Selected Poems: 1990-2010

Translated from the Italian by Marco Sonzogni

(An Italian-English Bilingual edition)

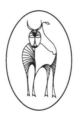

GUERNICA

TORONTO – BUFFALO – BERKELEY – LANCASTER (U.K.)

2012

Original titles:
Parabole smorzate (1999): Edizione Casagrande
Replica (2006): Edizione Casagrande

Michael Mirolla, editor
Guernica Editions Inc.
P.O. Box 117, Station P, Toronto (ON), Canada M5S 2S6
2250 Military Road, Tonawanda, N.Y. 14150-6000 U.S.A.

Distributors:
University of Toronto Press Distribution,
5201 Dufferin Street, Toronto (ON), Canada M3H 5T8
Gazelle Book Services, White Cross Mills, High Town, Lancaster LA1 4XS
U.K.
Small Press Distribution, 1341 Seventh St., Berkeley, CA 94710-1409
U.S.A.

First edition.
Printed in Canada.

Legal Deposit – Third Quarter
Library of Congress Catalog Card Number: 2012941656
Library and Archives Canada Cataloguing in Publication

De Marchi, Pietro
Here and not elsewhere : selected poems, 1990-2010 / Pietro De
Marchi ; Marco Sonzogni, translator.

(Essential translations series ; 7)
Issued also in electronic format.
Poems in Italian and English.
ISBN 978-1-55071-657-3

I. Title. II. Series: Essential translations series (Toronto, Ont.) ; 7.

PQ4864.E2222H47 2012   851'.914   C2012-904225-0

ACKNOWLEDGEMENTS

I would like to thank wholeheartedly the author,
Pietro De Marchi, for his encouragement and guidance.
Grateful thanks are also due to Michael Mirolla and Connie
McParland of Guernica Editions; to Fabio Casagrande and
Ilaria Antognoli of Edizioni Casagrande; to Barbara Rast and
Angelika Salvisberg of Pro Helvetia; and to Gabi Stöckli and
Monica Mutti of Übersetzerhaus Looren for their generosity
and assistance. To Anna Allenbach, Jackie Hemmingson,
Bob Lowe, Julia Maria Seemann and Ross Woods I am
indebted as ever for their support and advice. Special
thanks to Donal McLaughlin and Seraina Boner for their
companionship and conversations.

Contents

From *Replica / Response* (2006)

Appendix

Qui e non altrove

Che importa a questo punto
che in fondo al corridoio una finestra
inquadri tutto quanto il Resegone
e non come talvolta un disadorno
cortile d'ospedale? Eppure ha un senso
vederti proprio qui e non altrove, pensare
che il tuo viaggio, se termina, è qui,
accanto a questo grande
dipinto naturale.

Translator's Note

Da minha aldeia vejo quanto da terra se pode ver do Universo...
Por isso a minha aldeia é tão grande como outra terra qualquer,
porque eu sou do tamanho do que vejo
e não do tamanho da minha altura ...

— Fernando Pessoa, 'Liberdade'

Pietro De Marchi was born at Seregno (near Milan) in 1958. He graduated in literature at the University of Milan and this was followed by a doctorate at the University of Zurich. Since 1984 he has lived in Zurich, where he teaches Italian Literature as a *Titularprofessor* at the university. He also teaches as *professeur associé* at the University of Neuchatel (where he coordinates courses and seminars for the Master in Comparative Literature) and also at the University of Berne.

His publications include the edition of Francesco Bellati's *Poesie milanesi* (Milano: Schewiller, 1996) and two books of literary criticism: *Dove portano le parole. Sulla poesia di Giorgio Orelli e altro Novecento* (Lecce: Manni, 2002) and *Uno specchio di parole scritte. Da Parini a Pusterla, da Gozzi a Meneghello* (Firenze: Cesati, 2003). He has also edited (with Paolo Di Stefano) *Per Giorgio Orelli* (Bellinzona: Casagrande, 2001) and (with Giuliana Adamo) *Volta la carta la ze finia. Luigi Meneghello. Biografia per immagini* (Milano: Effigie, 2008).

He has recently curated (with Simone Soldini) the exhibition and the catalogue for *Giorgio Orelli. I giorni della vita* (Museo d'arte Mendrisio, Casa Croci, 1 September-13 November 2011). Since October 2010, he has been directing a research project into Swiss writers of prose in Italian for the Fondo Nazionale Svizzero. Currently he is editing *Lavori d'autunno*, a collection of short stories by Silvio Guarnieri (Lecce: Manni, 2012).

As a poet, De Marchi has published various pamphlets and two collections: *Parabole smorzate* and *Replica* (Bellinzona: Casagrande, 1999 and 2006). In 2007 *Replica* was awarded the *Premio della Fondazione Schiller*. In 2009 *Der Schwan und die Schaukel/Il cigno e l'altalena* appeared. This is a bilingual (Italian and German) anthology of his published and unpublished writing, edited and translated by Christoph Ferber (Zürich: Limmat Verlag).

In the introduction to De Marchi's first collection, Giorgio Orelli – the most distinguished Swiss poet writing in Italian – singled out "arguzia," wit, as the key characteristic of De Marchi's poetry: a poetry, as Orelli describes it, full of "roba scelta," of well-selected readings (from Orelli himself, from other Swiss poets like Fabio Pusterla, as well as from major European poets). And De Marchi's wit moves with deceiving subtleness from the unforgiving focus of his eye to the unassuming tone of his verse. Poised between a benevolent smile and a bitter grimace, De Marchi is always prepared to face the music of what happens and to recount it in "the language of all."

As De Marchi himself observes, "when we write we are alone and words are really what we have." This is why he tries to write poetry in ordinary language. This apparently unassuming standpoint actually camouflages De Marchi's commitment to the communicative power of poetry. Thus he patiently weaves believable narratives and emotions that are based on shared experiences yet enable him to explore his own individuality and realisations. De Marchi's disposition, though profoundly intellectual and rational, remains at all times open to the unexpected and the unknown and to their aesthetic and ethical implications.

The poems that follow – selected by the poet himself from published as well as unpublished or uncollected work – represent the variety of De Marchi's poetry. This is a poet who speaks clearly, who does not indulge in half-hearted exchanges, and who is willing to read between the lines. This is a poet who relishes the here and now and the epiphany possible in every moment – a poet who is therefore ready to seize and share what is *here and not elsewhere*. Reading De Marchi, one is reminded of Pessoa's predicament:

> From my village I see how much of the earth we can see from the Universe …
> that's why my village is as big as any other one,
> because I'm as high as the things I see
> and not as high as my height.

This anthology represents two decades of poetry: the mapped universe of a poet whose measured voice and understated language are a constant challenge to the translator. I have responded to the challenge by seizing and sharing the stories and the emotions of the author.

Marco Sonzogni

FROM PARABOLE SMORZATE / LOBS (1999)

Parabole smorzate

Se l'avversario è più forte che mai
se con urlo strozzato si avventa sulla palla
e affonda di diritto
e incrocia col rovescio a due mani
tu non lo assecondare nel gioco a fondo campo
perché alla lunga ti sfiata ti spompa e alla fine
non avrai scampo un suo passante
ti infilerà

Tu invece rompi il suo ritmo
smorza la palla, liftala, dàlle
più effetto che puoi
fa' che ricada appena al di là della
rete.

Lobs

If your opponent is stronger than ever
if with a strangled cry he goes for the ball
and attacks with a deep forehand
and a cross-court, two-hand backhand
don't indulge in baseline play
because in the long run you'll be out of breath and in the end
you won't have a show, one of his passing shots
will beat you

Instead, break his rhythm
lob, spin the ball
as much as you can
so that it drops on just the other side of the
net.

Capriccio

Si fa di celluloide il mondo fuori,
voci doppiate, grida soffocate
dallo schermo di vetro ...
È un istante, poi tutto

si appiattisce, ripiombi
nel sonno, nel *sueño* ...
Il mondo si dilegua in verticale:
e allora gufi, pipistrelli,

un cane che è un gatto
e altri effetti speciali, prevalenza del nero.
Ma la mano che ti scuote, la voce

che ti chiama («Su dài, dobbiamo scendere»)
è la mano del mondo e la sua voce
vera.

Capricho

The outer world is made of celluloid,
dubbed voices, choked cries
from the glass screen ...
It's an instant, then all

goes flat, you plunge back
into sleep, in *sueño* ...
The world vanishes upwards:
and then owls, bats,

a dog that is a cat
and other special effects, black predominates.
But the hand that shakes you, the voice

that calls you ("Come on, we've got to go down")
is the hand of the world and its real
voice.

The title alludes to one of Goya's *caprichos*: the etching where the mind's dreamful
sleep generates monsters ("el sueño de la razón produce monstrous").

Con Valentina, dalle anatre

I

L'hanno vista arrivare
col sacchetto di plastica
e a gara tutte insieme (tranne *Fritzli*)
le sono corse incontro sulla neve.
È la nonna delle anatre:
è lei che ha dato il nome a *Fritzli*,
l'anatra che zoppica.

II

Sì, zoppica, lo vedi anche da te:
bisogna che qualcuno se ne occupi.
Se vola non si nota,
e neppure se nuota,
ma ora sul laghetto
c'è una crosta di ghiaccio
e due dita di neve.

III

Ricordi, l'anno scorso,
quell'anatra che aveva il becco storto?
Spezzavi il pane in pezzi piccolissimi,
poi le andavi *vicino vicinissimo*,
vincendo la paura.

With Valentina, where the ducks are

I

They saw her coming
with a plastic bag
and all together (except *Fritzli*) vied
to run to her over the snow.
She's the ducks' grannie:
she's the one that named *Fritzli*,
the limping duck.

II

Yes, she limps, and you can see it for yourself:
somebody has to take care of her.
When she flies, you don't notice,
or when she swims,
but now on the pond
there's a crust of ice
and two inches of snow.

III

Do you remember, last year,
that duck with the bent beak?
You broke the bread in very small pieces,
then you went *so close, so very close* to her,
overcoming fear.

Eliminare il superfluo

Eliminare il superfluo, gettare
la zavorra, sgombrare
gli impacci, gli intralci, strappare
le erbacce, estirpare
il convolvolo, fare
piazza pulita, tabula rasa.

Poi spogliarsi del troppo e del vano,
ridurre all'osso, scarnire, spolpare,
lasciare
soltanto l'essenziale.

Throw away what's not needed

Throw away what's not needed; chuck out the
ballast; clear
hindrances, obstacles; pull out
weeds; root out
bindweed; clean the
house from top to botton; make a clean sweep of it all.

Then rid yourself of vain excess;
become bone-bare, flesh-free;
leave
only what's essential.

Qui sopra dove c'è lo spazio bianco

Qui sopra dove c'è lo spazio bianco
mettete pure il tempo che è passato,
con quello che comporta, c'è bisogno
di entrare nei dettagli?, case vuote
o vendute, lavori di ampliamento
laggiù sulla collina...

Quello che è bianco è bianco
oppure è cancellato.

Over here where there's white space

Over here where there's white space
feel free to put down the time spent
and what it entails, you don't need
details, do you? houses emptied
or sold, extension work
down there on the hill...

What's white is white
or else is wiped.

Una pagina di cielo

«Scrivere ordinatamente
una pagina di cielo
e una di cieco»
(dal *Diario di seconda*, 1965-66)

Qui ci vorrebbe un pennello cinese.
I colori sarebbero il bianco del foglio
(questo cielo di ovatta)
ed il nero di china
(quel nero di nubi laggiù).

«Se oggi seren non è,
doman seren sarà.
Se non sarà seren,
si rasserenerà».

Forse è meglio aspettare.
Più sereni domani
scriveremo una pagina intera,
di un cielo non cieco,
con la più bella delle biro blu.

A page of sky

> "To fill
> a page wlth 'sky'
> and another page with 'blind'"
> (from *Primary School Diary Year 2*, 1965-66)

Here, we would need a Chinese brush
The colours would be the white of the page
(this cotton wool sky)
And the black of the Chinese ink
(black like the clouds over there)

"If it isn't sunny today,
to-morrow will be better.
If it isn't better then,
it will be one day."

Some times it is better to wait.
Better to-morrow
we will fill a whole page
with sky that isn't blind
in a lovely blue biro.

A common spelling exercise in Italian primary schools is for a child to write down
the word *cielo* (sky) or *cieco* (blind) many times.

Immaginate una coppia ...

Immaginate una coppia di anziani ciclisti,
lui che è in testa a dettare l'andatura
e ogni tanto si volta a controllare
compreso del suo ruolo d'apripista,

lei che è a ruota e pedala concentrata, le mani
ben strette sul manubrio.
Ed ora immaginate lei che a un tratto

si rialza sulla sella, esita un attimo

stacca una mano, l'altra, dal manubrio e prova,
come fosse la prima volta prova
ad andare senza mani.

Immaginate, immaginate, intanto
io li vedo qui davanti
pedalare come in gara contro il tempo.

Imagine a pair of …

Imagine a pair of old cyclists
the one in front setting the pace
and full of himself as fore runner
every so often he turns to check

the one behind who pedals fixedly, hands
tight on the handlebars.
And, now, imagine, she suddenly
lifts herself off the saddle, hesitates for an instant,

takes one hand, then the other off the handlebar
and tries, like it was for the first time, and tries
to ride no hands.

Imagine, imagine, meanwhile,
I see them pedalling away
as if they were racing time.

Rettili

Se solo potessero
farebbero sogni di un lusso
sfrenato, avere due code
o vivere a Capri,

o sogni concreti, da mordere,
da masticare,
una formica, una vespa stecchita,
un'ala di cicala,

o anche sogni più tetri,
un'ombra sul sasso,
un fischio nell'aria, poi il senso
di qualcosa che manca.

Ma i rettili non sognano.
È questione di sangue: freddo.

Reptiles

If only they could
they would dream dreams
of unbridled luxury: of having two tails
or of living in Capri,

or dreams of substance, to bite,
to chew,
an ant, a stone-dead wasp,
the wing of a cicada,

or darker dreams,
shadow against stone,
whistle in the air, then the sense
of something missing.

But reptiles don't do dreams.
It's their blood, being cold.

L'entomologo

Con lo spillino trafigge l'insetto
appena catturato,
poi sotto
vi incolla il cartellino
col nome e altri dati.
Così – beato –
tra le parole e le cose
riduce lo iato.

The entomologist

He runs a pin through the insect
newly caught,
then further down
he sticks a label
with its name and other facts.
Thus – bless him –
he abridges the gulf between
words and things.

Conflans

Passa una chiatta che porta carbone,
ma è troppo lontana,
non riesco a leggerne il nome.
Ero venuto a cercare una nave in disarmo,
ho chiesto in giro, non mi sanno dire,
non c'è nessuna *Destinée* da queste parti.
Ma io ho fiducia, io l'aspetto, forse
il suo nome adesso ce l'ha
una chiatta che porta carbone.

Conflans

A coal barge passes,
but too far away,
for me to read its name.
I'd come here to look for a laid up ship,
I've asked around, they don't know,
there's no *Destinée* around here.
But I've got faith, I'll wait for her, perhaps
even now, her name is on
a coal barge.

Foto di paesaggio con figure

Il paesaggio, per me, può stare sullo sfondo.
Qui a Bergen, per esempio,
lo spettacolo è il mare con le dune,
non c'è niente da dire ...

Eppure mi distraggo e guardo i passeri,
una dozzina almeno attavolati
due tavoli più in là, fanno lo slalom
fra tazze, cucchiaini e briciole di toast.

Di tanto in tanto guardo anche la donna
che è al tavolo dei passeri e non bada
ai passeri e agli sguardi e guarda il mare.

Per discrezione metto a fuoco i passeri,
ma inquadro anche la donna
e dietro a lei le dune e dietro il mare.

Photo of landscape with figures

The landscape, for me, can be in the background.
Here in Bergen, for instance,
the spectacle is sea with dunes,
no comment ...

Yet I am distracted and I watch the sparrows,
a dozen of them at least landed on a table
two tables away, they dodge between
cups, teaspoons and toastcrumbs.

Every now and then I also look at the woman
who's sitting at the table with the sparrows and doesn't mind
the sparrows or being stared at, and she looks at the sea.

To be discreet I gaze at the sparrows,
but also I focus on the woman
and beyond her the dunes and beyond the dunes the sea.

Verso Marina

Rischia grosso il ramarro maremmano
se sotto la gran fersa dell'estate
attraversa la pista
ciclabile e non vede
la ruota che si arresta,
e non legge il cartello che ripete
per l'ennesima volta la minaccia:
PROBABILE CADUTA RAMI E PIGNE.

Io, ciclista alfabeta,
mi affido al dio del caso, se mi assiste,
sfido l'azzardo di una
pineta minata dall'alto,
sotto una pioggia di aghi
riparto, riprendo il mio ritmo
pronto allo scarto,
al rapido zig zag
o alla frenata brusca
per ramarri che cambiano siepe,
per rami o pigne in libera
caduta.

Towards Marina

In Maremma the green lizard really sticks his neck out
when whipped on by the heat of summer
it crosses the bicycle
path and doesn't see
the wheel that comes to a halt,
and doesn't read the sign that threatens
for the umpteenth time:
DANGER – FALLING BRANCHES AND PINE CONES.

I, being a literate cyclist,
trust to the god of chance, if he is on my side,
I brave the dangers of a
pine forest booby-trapped from above,
under a shower of needles
I get going again, I get back into my rhythm
ready for the swerve,
for the swift zig zag
or the sudden stop
for green lizards that swap hedges,
or for branches or pine cones in free
fall.

Marina di Grosseto is a seaside town near Grosseto in the Maremma – a territory between
Tuscany and Lazio, in central Italy, facing the sea. The green lizard has a strong literary
pedigree: De Marchi follows Dante (*Inf.*, XXV 79-81: "Come 'l ramarro sotto la gran
fersa / del dì canicular cangiando sepe, / folgore par se la via attraversa"; "Just as the
lizard, when it darts from hedge / to hedge, beneath the dog days' giant lash, / seems, if
it cross one's path, a lightning flash" in Allen Mandelbaum's translation: *The Comedy of
Dante Alighieri: Inferno*, 1980) and Montale (*Le occasioni*, 1939: "Il ramarro, se scocca /
sotto la grande fersa / dalle stoppie"; "The green lizard, if it streaks / through stubble / in
the stifling heat" in Stephen Yenser's translation: *Corno inglese. An anthology of Eugenio
Montale's poetry in English translation*, 2009).

All'angolo di Freiestrasse

Basta poco, un cappello nero, un nero cappotto
(niente di strano a queste latitudini),
e un uomo studia il passo, ti raggiunge
e d'un fiato *Raphèl maí amècche* comincia a dire...

Tu non capisci, non rispondi, lo deludi
e un dubbio allora lo punge
che quasi già un dubbio non è,
cambia lingua, domanda: *Sind Sie Jude?*

In quell'istante, sul suo viso perplesso
(non puoi dire: semita),
leggi l'ansia di un uomo in fuga da tutta una vita.

Tu pensi: il tempo passa,
la storia si ripete o lascia strascichi.
Lui già saluta e imbocca Freiestrasse.

At the corner of Freiestrasse

It doesn't take much, a black hat, a black coat
(nothing unusual round here),
and a man quickens his step, catches up with you
and breathlessly begins to say *Raphèl maì amècche* ...

You don't get it, you don't answer, you dismay him
and so a doubt that is no longer
a doubt bothers him,
he switches languages, he asks: *Sind Sie Jude?*

In that moment, in his puzzled face
(you mustn't say, Semitic),
you see the anxiety of man rushing all his life.

You think: time goes by,
history repeats itself or leaves traces.
He is already saying goodbye and goes down Freiestrasse.

Freiestrasse s is a street in Zurich, Switzerland, not far from where the poet lives.
Raphèl maì amèche zabí almi is a verse from Dante's Commedia, *Inf.* XXXI 67:
"'Raphèl maì amècche zabì almi,' / cominciò a gridar la fiera bocca, / cui non si
convenia più dolci salmi" ("'Raphael mai amech izabi almi,' / began to clamour
the ferocious mouth, / to which were not befitting sweeter psalms" in Allen
Mandelbaum's translation: *The Divine Comedy of Dante Alighieri: Inferno*, 1980). The
verse is shouted out by Nimrod, who is a demonic giant in Dante's epic poem but
not one in Biblical texts. In German "Sind Sie Jude?" means "Are you a Jew?"

Frontespizio

Livros são papéis pintados com tinta
— Fernando Pessoa

Ma chi lo dice
che la carta è felice
quando annusa nell'aria questo odore
di inchiostro? Sarà vero
che la titilla il solletico
delle mie dita?
Chi ci assicura che non ha paura
di una matita ben appuntita?
Chi lo sa cosa prova
quando una penna la sfiora,
magari si dispera
nel vedersi allo specchio
gli scarabocchi, gli sgorbi, le macchie.
Non ha poi grandi pretese,
la carta, come tutti
vuole arrivare alla fine del mese.
Forse il suo sogno sarebbe di vivere
in santa pace così come è nata,
bianca immacolata,
per poi sparire
non appena incomincia ad ingiallire.

Frontispiece

Livros são papéis pintados com tinta
— Fernando Pessoa

But who's to say
if the paper is happy
when it gets a whiff
of ink in the air? Can it be true
that it gets a thrill
from my caressing fingers?
Who can reassure us that it is unafraid
of a well-sharpened pencil?
Who knows what it feels
when a pen scratches it,
perhaps it agonizes
when it sees in the mirror
the scribbles, scrawls, and stains all over itself.
It has no big expectations after all,
paper, like everybody else
just wants to get by.
Perhaps its dream would be to live
as peacefully as it was born,
white immaculate,
and then to disappear
as soon as it starts to go yellow.

In Patricia Vasconcelos Cavalcanti's translation the quotation – from 'Liberdade' (1935), one of Pessoa's most well-known poems and a hymn to human freedom – reads as: "[b]ooks are painted papers."

Il cigno e l'altalena

È fermo eppure dondola
il cigno che lento si liscia
sull'acqua di raso del lago:
lo sospinge una bava

di vento, lo raggiunge
impercettibile l'onda.
Transita al largo un kayak,
i soliti passeri a riva

saltellano, perlustrano la ghiaia.
L'alternativo con cane si allena
a lanciare in aria il bastone

per riprenderlo al volo.
Intanto tu vai dallo scivolo
all'altalena.

The swan and the swing

The swan is still, yet swings
and slowly slides
on the smooth shaven water
of the lake:

a froth of wind wafts it on,
the wave barely touches it.
A kayak crosses the lake,
as usual the sparrows hop

on the shore, patrolling the shingle.
Someone trendy practices
throwing a stick up in the air

for his dog to catch.
In the meantime you go from the slide
to the swing.

This is the title poem of De Marchi's selected works in Christoph Ferber's German
translation: *Der Schwan und die Schaukel. Gedichte und Prosastücke 1990-2008.*

Maturità senz'altra forza atterra

(da Danilo Kiš)

D'autunno quando i venti
si levano le foglie dei castagni
cadono a capofitto, col picciolo
in giù. Si sente un tocco,
è come se un uccello
cadesse sulla terra
col becco.
                Ma da sola
cade la castagna,
senza bisogno del vento.

Ripeness falls of itself

(from Danilo Kiš)

In autumn when the winds blow
the leaves of chestnut trees
fall headlong, stem first.
You hear a tap,
it is as if a bird
hit the ground
beak first.
             But a chestnut
falls by itself,
with no need for the wind.

Danilo Kiš (1935-1989) was a Yugoslavian novelist, short story writer and poet who wrote in Serbo-Croatian. Kiš was influenced by Bruno Schulz, Vladimir Nabokov, and Jorge Luis Borges.

Amarillide

Prima che il tuo incanto sfiorisca,
Belladonna dalle ciglia color zafferano,
prima che l'incarnato
dei tuoi gigli avvizzisca

prestami le tue verdi sciabole,
carnose penne d'oca da gigante,
insegnami Amarillide a scrivere
voci che tacciano e trilli del diavolo.

Amaryllis

Before the charm withers of your
saffron-eyed deadly nightshade
before the charm wilts
of your lilies

lend me your green sabres,
your fleshy giant goose quills,
Amaryllis, show me how to write
with silent voices and the devil's trills.

Amaryllis is a small genus of flowering bulbs, with two species, the better known
of which is *Amaryllis belladonna*, native to South Africa. Plants of this genus are
also known as *amarillo, belladonna lily*, or *naked lady* (because of the plant's pattern
of flowering – usually white with crimson veins but also pink or purple – when the
foliage has died down). Amaryllis is also a character in Milton's *Lycidas*: "To sport
with Amaryllis in the shade / or in the tangles of Neaera's hair" (Milton is referring
to indulging in routine worldly pleasures).

Non vedi non senti non parli

Non vedi non senti non parli
ma nuoti, nel mare
amniotico ti immergi
riemergi, sono cento-
cinquantasei i tuoi battiti

Che batticuore vederti che nuoti
ci sei, non lo sai, sei
sei centimetri e nuoti

See no evil, hear no evil, speak no evil

You can't see you can't hear you can't speak
but you can swim, in the amniotic
sea you sink down
come up, your heartbeats are
one hundred and fifty six.

How my heart beats, to see you swim
you are, you don't know it,
you are two inches under and you swim

The original title of the poem echoes the three wise monkeys (in Japanese
san'en or *sanzaru*, or *sanbiki no saru*, literally "three monkeys"), also called the three
mystic apes: a pictorial maxim embodying the proverbial principle to "see no evil,
hear no evil, speak no evil." Since the poem talks about the developing fœtus of the
poet's daughter – life still poised between being (the fœtus exists and swims) and the
unawareness of its being (the newborn exists but it does not know it yet) – it seemed
appropriate to capture this pre-natal innocence by combining a literal translation of
the title with the Japanese exhortation to maintain an uncontaminated conduct.

Cézanne

Questa tela grigia
questa pera gialla
questa melagrana
questa brocca d'acqua.

Era frutta matura sul piatto,
è una natura morta con frutta.

Cézanne

This grey canvas
this yellow pear
this pomegranate
this jug of water.

It was ripe fruit on a plate,
it is a still life with fruit.

The poem is a respectful parody of 'Canto beduino' ('Bedouin Song', 1932), a poem
by the Italian poet Giuseppe Ungaretti (1888-1970).

Come Cechov

Penso a Carver, Raymond
Carver di Clatskanie, Oregon.
Sto leggendo *Errand*, la short story
che scrisse nell'ultimo anno
che visse. Racconta di Cechov che muore,
racconta di Carver che muore. Come
Cechov voleva scrivere Raymond
Carver di Clatskanie, Oregon.

Like Chekhov

I think of Carver, Raymond
Carver of Clatskanie, Oregon.
I'm reading *Errand*, the short story
he wrote in the last year
of his life. It talks about Chekhov dying,
it talks about Carver dying. Like Chekhov
wanted to write Raymond
Carver of Clatskanie, Oregon.

The short story writer and poet Raymond Clevie Carver jr (1938-1988) is a major figure in 20th century American literature and is credited with revitalizing the short story in the 1980s. 'Errand' was published in *The New Yorker* on June 1, 1987 (p. 30), a little over a year before Carver's death on August 2, 1988. Clatskanie is a mill town near the Columbia river, in Oregon.

FROM REPLICA / RESPONSE (2006)

Cambi di marcia

... perché il viaggio contempla
ampi tratti in pianura, autostradali
ma anche strettoie repentine, curve
a gomito, una serie infinita di tornanti,
poi rampe ponti sottopassi tunnel ...

Gear Shifts

… because the trip means
long stretches of flat, highwayed land
but also sudden bottlenecks,
elbows, endless rounds of hairpin bends,
then ramps bridges underpasses tunnels …

Inganno ottico

Se l'aquilastro o falco pescatore
naturalmente fa quel che l'istinto gli detta e librandosi alto
si lascia trasportare dal vento, poi plana roteando
e sceso a pelo d'acqua per un attimo increspa
la superficie del lago, a pesca di coregoni o di persici,
provando e riprovando finché la fortuna l'assista nel becco;
se qualcuno ti presta il binocolo
e mentre guardi ti pare ad un tratto che il falco
con le larghe ali tese si schianti
contro i balconi balaustrati della riva opposta,
quasi subito sai che si tratta di un banale inganno ottico,
di un effetto di schiacciamento della prospettiva,
perché in realtà quel che conta e ti attrae
accade in mezzo al lago, non ha niente da spartire
con le dimore patrizie, il ghiaietto dei viali, i motoscafi
d'alto bordo ormeggiati nei garage.

Optical illusion

If the sea eagle or fish hawk
naturally does what instinct tells it and hovering high
lets itself be carried by the wind, then glides circling
and drops to an inch from the water for a moment it ripples
the surface of the lake, fishing for tench or perch,
over and over again till luck rewards it and its beak;
if someone lends you their binoculars
and as you watch it suddenly looks to you as though the hawk
with its large wings spread out were about to crash
against the railed balconies on the opposite shore,
almost immediately you know it for just an optical illusion,
a distorted perspective,
because what really matters and attracts you
happens out in the middle of the lake, has nothing to do with
patrician houses, the gravelled paths, the tall
motorboats moored by the garage.

Una sovrapposizione per Giampiero Neri

Grande quanto un gufo reale
la civetta delle nevi (*Nyctea scandiaca*)
ruotava il capo arruffando le penne.
Ma non vedeva niente,
neanche un topo in fuga.
Non c'era niente,
tranne il bianco perenne.

An overlap for Giampiero Neri

As big as an eagle owl
the white owl (*Nyctea scandiaca*)
would rotate her head, feathers ruffling.
But she couldn't see anything,
not even a fleeing mouse.
There was nothing,
except for the eternal blankness.

In an essay on poetics, 'Sovrapposizione di Storia e Natura nella ricerca letteraria' ('History and Nature Overlap in Literary Research,' in *Kamen*, 19, 2002), the Italian poet and critic Giampiero Neri (Giampiero Pontiggia, 1927) examines how human history and animal history are similar. Neri maintains that the behaviour of humans and of animals overlap: in this poem, such overlap involves a snow owl (Linnæus, 1758) and the poet's octogenarian grandfather, who looks around and finds that his lifelong friends have all died.

Lettera da Binz

a Fabio Pusterla

Dalle parti del maneggio
dove c'è quella pista d'atletica senza reti né cancelli
dove il tartan è d'un rosso così rosso
che pensi a un'anguria matura
dove l'erba del prato è d'un verde così verde
che non osi calpestarla
è lì che sosto, tutti i mercoledì,
nell'ora che mia figlia va a cavallo.
Ma l'altra settimana
lì c'erano i ragazzi delle scuole: s'allenavano,
saltavano, correvano nel sole.
Oggi invece la pista era in mano ai soldati,
tutti armati, non tutti fino ai denti:
qualcuno s'aggirava nei dintorni
misurando, fissando a terra pioli, cavi del telefono;
ai piedi d'un castagno altri parlavano
a un compagno nascosto tra le foglie;
appaiati, due caccia
sfrecciavano nel cielo, verso est,
poi tornavano indietro col frastuono consueto.
S'avvertiva un disagio, un principio di paura.
Forse per questo un soldato passando mi ha detto: *Grüezi*.

Quando fu tempo di tornare al maneggio
lungo la strada ho raccolto una pera caduta: la parte
non marcia era d'un dolce
troppo dolce da dire.

The Swiss-German greeting "Grüezi" is equivalent to the standard German "Grüss Gott".

50

Letter from Binz

to Fabio Pusterla

Near the horse riding school
where there's that running track with no fences or gates
where the track surface is red so red
that you think of a ripe water-melon
where the grass of the lawn is green so green
that you don't dare to tread on it
that's where I hang about, every Wednesday
when my daughter goes horse riding.
But the other week
there were kids from school there; they were training,
they were jumping and running in the sun.
Today, however, the track was taken over by soldiers,
all armed, but not all of them armed to the teeth:
one was hanging about
pacing off then pegging out telephone cables;
at the foot of a chestnut, others were talking
to a comrade hidden up in the leaves;
paired off, two fighters
roared through the sky, towards the East,
then they turned back, with the usual din.
There was a sense of unease, a feeling of fear.
Perhaps that was why a passing soldier said to me: G'day.

When it was time to go back to the riding school,
along the way I picked up a wind-fall pear; the bit
not rotten was sweet,
too sweet to describe.

Binz is a little village near Zürich, Switzerland.

51

Davanti alla Pinacoteca

... how it takes place
while someone else is eating ...
     W.H. Auden, 'Musée des Beaux Arts'

Seduto a un tavolo del bar all'angolo
tra Brera e Fiori Chiari,
guardi e ascolti la vita quotidiana.
C'è chi racconta storie sue o d'altri,
storie di figli, di mariti e mogli.
C'è chi si fa spiegare la divina proporzione
perché ha l'esame questo pomeriggio
e ancora non la sa.
Quando passa un ragazzo un po' artista nel vestire,
si volta una ragazza e dice cazzo!, me ne sono innamorata.
In quel momento suona il cellulare: è sua madre,
l'hanno detto alla radio.
C'è chi da un altro tavolo s'informa:
sì, a Londra, stamattina, delle bombe nel metrò.
C'è chi arriva solo ora e non sa niente,
si siede, dà un'occhiata alla carta, poi ordina
vino bianco e prosciutto col melone.

In front of the art gallery

... how it takes place
while someone else is eating ...
W.H. Auden, 'Musée des Beaux Arts'

Seated at a table in the bar on the corner
between Brera and Fiori Chiari
you look on and listen in to every day life.
There's someone telling stories about himself or other people,
stories about kids, husbands or wives.
There's some one explaining the Golden Section
because he's got an exam that afternoon
and still he can't get it.
Then a youth dressed a bit arty comes by,
and up jumps a girl and says: "Fuck! I am in love with him."
Just then, her mobile rings: it is her mother,
it is on the radio.
There's some one from another table who's finding out:
yes, in London, this morning, bombs in the Underground.
There's someone who has just arrived and knows nothing
about it,
he sits down, glances at the menu and then orders
ham and melon with a white wine.

The Pinacoteca di Brera (established between 1773 and 1776 by Queen Maria
Theresa of Austria) is a well-known art gallery in central Milan and borders via Brera
and via Fiori Chiari. The golden section (from the Latin *sectio aurea*) – also referred
to as golden ratio or divine proportion – is a rule about the aesthetics of proportion
(the poet is familiar with Luca Pacioli's *De divina proportione* (1497), an illuminating
treatise on the golden section in art history). The epigraph is from an ekphrastic
poem by W.H. Auden (1907-1973) based on Pieter Brueghel's *Landscape with The Fall
of Icarus* (ca 1560?, oil on canvas, 73.5 x 112 cm) in Brussels' Museum of Fine Arts.
De Marchi alludes to the fatal London Underground bombings in 2005.

Anni Settanta

Qui la storia del Carmagnola comincia ad esser legata con quella del suo tempo.
Alessandro Manzoni

Fu sotto i portici dell'Arengario
che la sua storia cominciò a legarsi
con quella del suo tempo.
Ne uscì manganellato, l'occhio nero,
quattro punti, un grave stato
confusionale. All'ospedale
il commissario chiese
se era dei rossi o dei neri, poi disse:
la politica, sa, l'è roba sporca.
Come fare a spiegargli che passava
di lì per caso, andava in piazza Diaz
per via di una ricerca,
aveva quindici anni,
era al ginnasio…

The Seventies

*Qui la storia del Carmagnola comincia ad esser legata con
quella del suo tempo.*
Alessandro Manzoni

It was under the Arengario arches
that his story began to link itself
to the history of his time.
He came out beaten up, a black eye,
four stiches, severe
concussion. At the hospital
the policeman asked
was he one of the reds or the blacks, then said:
politics, you know, it's a dirty business.
How could he tell the cop that he was walking
there by chance, he was going across piazza Diaz
for a research project,
he was fifteen
he was in high school ...

In Federica Brunori Deigan's translation, the quotation – from Manzoni's historical
introduction to his play *Il Conte di Carmagnola* (1820; *The Count of Carmagnola*,
2004) – reads as: "Here the story of Carmagnola begins to be linked to the history of
his time." The arches (Arengario) and the square (Piazza Diaz) are in central Milan,
near the Cathedral (Duomo).

Attraversando la Polonia

... *rosseggiavano lontani i campanili di Cracovia.*
Primo Levi, *La tregua*

Pecore, capre, cavalli.
Un uomo che munge una vacca in mezzo a un prato.
Bambini che corrono per guardare il treno che passa.
Ci si ferma in una stazione.
Non c'è quasi il tempo di accorgersi che siamo a O.
Case, antenne paraboliche, come altrove.
Si riparte.
Riprendo la lettura del mio libro.
Nie rozumiem po polsku.
Non capisco il polacco.

Travelling through Poland

...rosseggiavano lontani i campanili di Cracovia.
Primo Levi, *La tregua*

Sheep, goats, horses.
A man milks a cow in the middle of a meadow.
Children run to watch the train go by.
We stop at a station.
Almost no time to notice we are in O.
Houses, satellite dishes, like elsewhere.
We get going again.
I go back to my book.
Nie rozumiem po polsku.
I don't understand Polish.

In Stuart Woolf's translation of *La tregua* (1963; *The Truce*, 1965) the quotation reads as: "in the distance the red of Krakow's belltowers." "O" is the initial of Oświęcim, the Polish name for Auschwitz. As the last line of the poem explains, in Polish "Nie rozumiem po polsku" – which Levi mentions in *La tregua* – means: "I don't understand Polish."

Promemoria da un luogo di betulle

per Katia Bleier Meneghello

Ogni volta che corri alla finestra
per distrarre la mente dalla vista
di quello che rimane dei sommersi,
lì fuori trovi sempre una betulla,

il prato, i fiori gialli, il cielo terso.
Potessimo bandire il nostro tempo,
tornare indietro a inizio Novecento,
qui avremmo solo un bosco di betulle,

le strade, qualche casa, la tranquilla
estate dei paesi di pianura.
Ma niente più cancella quei capelli

tosati, quegli occhiali di metallo,
quelle povere scarpe color polvere:
quello che non fu cenere, né fumo.

Note from a birch wood

for Katia Bleier Meneghello

Every time that you run to the window
to distract your mind from seeing
what remains of the slaughtered,
outside you always find a birch tree,

the grass, the yellow flowers, the gleaming sky.
If only we could wipe out our time
and go back to the beginning of the 20th century
when all we had was a copse of birches,

the roads, a few houses, calm
summer in the villages of the plain.
But nothing can erase those shaven

heads, those metallic eyes
those poor dust coloured shoes;
stuff that is neither ashes nor smoke.

The title of the poem – "luogo di bettulle," literally "place of birch trees" – alludes to the small
Polish town of Brzezinka, Birkenau in German, where the Nazis built the concentration camp
(the "ashes" and "smoke" of the last line are ominously evocative and revealing). The poem
also alludes to *Promemoria* (1994), a book about the extermination of European Jews during
World War II by Luigi Meneghello (1922-2007), a renowned Italian writer and academic
who was the first Professor of Italian Studies at the University of Reading (UK). Katia Bleier
Meneghello (1918-2004) was Meneghello's wife. Born in Yugoslavia (Ba ka Vojvodina) into
a Magyar-speaking Jewish family, Katia grew up in Zagreb until she was forced to flee in 1941
following the German invasion. In 1944, with her parents and other relatives, she was taken to
Auschwitz and then to Bergen-Belsen, and was freed by the Allies in 1945, believing herself
to be the only survivor in her family. In 1947, having discovered that her sister Olga had also
survived and was now living in North-Eastern Italy, Katia went as a clandestine migrant to
Malo, near Vicenza, the birthplace of her future husband Luigi, whom she married in 1948. De
Marchi has written extensively on the work of Luigi Meneghello and, with Giuliana Adamo,
is the editor of *Volta la carta la ze finia. Luigi Meneghello. Biografia per immagini* (Milano: Effigie,
2008), a photobiography of the writer.

Funerale a Baar

quando fra un treno e l'altro un colombo si posa sulle rotaie
Giorgio Orelli, 'In ripa di Tesino'

Mentre in chiesa il pastore legge e spiega
la prima delle *Lettere ai Corinzi*
con quello *speculum* e quell'*ænigmate*
e il conoscere e l'esser conosciuti,

come impone l'orario, puntuali
fuori passano i treni, poi ripassano
non lontani dal prato suburbano
dove il compianto già riposa in pace.

Parenti e amici ascoltano compunti
il *nunc* e il *tunc*, il *facie ad faciem*,
solo una donna è scossa da un singulto.

Ma nessuno là fuori sa fermare
il regolare transito dei treni,
quel rumore di ruote, di rotaie.

Funeral at Baar

quando fra un treno e l'altro un colombo si posa sulle rotaie
Giorgio Orelli, 'In ripa di Tesino'

While in church the pastor reads out and then explains
the *First Letter to the Corinthians*
with *speculum* and *ænigmate*
and knowing and being known,

as arranged by the time-table, the trains
outside pass punctually, then they go by again
quite near the suburban lawns
where the departed already rests in peace.

Relatives and friends listen with reverence to
nunc and *tunc*, to *facie ad faciem*,
only one lady shakes with sobs.

But nobody outside can shut down
the regular passing of the trains
that noise of wheels, of rails.

Baar is a village in the canton of Zug, Switzerland. The quotation from Orelli's poem
reads as: "when a pigeon settles on the rails between one train and the next" (my
translation). The Latin words are from 1 Corinthians 13:12: "Cernimus enim nunc
per speculum in ænigmate: tunc autem facie ad faciem: nunc cognosco ex parte:
tune vero cognoscam, quem admodum et cognitus sum" ("For now we see through a
glass, darkly; but then face to face: now I know in part; but then shall I know even
as also I am known").

Qui e non altrove

Che importa a questo punto
che in fondo al corridoio una finestra
inquadri tutto quanto il Resegone
e non come talvolta un disadorno
cortile d'ospedale? Eppure ha un senso
vederti proprio qui e non altrove, pensare
che il tuo viaggio, se termina, è qui,
accanto a questo grande
dipinto naturale.

Here and not elsewhere

What does it matter at this stage
that at the end of the corridor a window
frames the entire Resegone range
and not, as sometimes happens, a bare
hospital courtyard? Yet it makes sense
to see you here and not somewhere else, to think
that your journey, if it's coming to an end, it's here,
near this grand
natural landscape.

The Resegone is a mountain range in the North-Western Alps of Italy between the
county of Bergamo and Lecco, in Lombardy. The origin of the name – *resega*, the
Lombard dialect word for saw – is from the nine peaks of the range, as Alessandro
Manzoni's famously explains in the opening page of his historical novel, *I promessi
sposi* (1827-1840; *The Betrothed*, 1834): "La costiera, formata dal deposito di tre grossi
torrenti, scende appoggiata a due monti contigui, l'uno detto di san Martino, l'altro,
con voce lombarda, il *Resegone*, dai molti suoi cocuzzoli in fila, che in vero lo fanno
somigliare a una sega" ("The bank, formed by the deposit of three large mountain
streams, descends from the bases of two contiguous mountains, the one called St.
Martin, the other by a Lombard name, *Resegone*, from its long line of summits, which
in truth give it the appearance of a saw" in Count O'Mahony's translation).

Variazioni su un tema antico

Dove saranno a quest'ora Vilmante,
la bella lituana, e Arneta e le altre?
E la più dolce di tutte, Ljudmila ucraina,

che un giorno di settembre, a Berlino,
chiedendole io se il marito,
di cui parlava spesso all'imperfetto,

sarebbe presto venuto a trovarla,
con un filo di voce mi disse
«Mein Mann... ist... vermisst».

«Quel giorno uscì di casa e poi nessuno,
più nessuno da allora l'ha visto.
Sono quattordici mesi che aspetto

notizie, che aspettiamo, io e Klarina,
ma lei è così piccola, non credo
che potrà ricordare».

Dove saranno a quest'ora Vilmante,
la bella lituana, e Arneta e le altre?
Ljudmila, dovunque tu sia,

perdona se ti ho messa in poesia.

Variations on an ancient theme

Where now is Vilmante,
the lovely Lithuanian, and Arneta and the others?
And the loveliest of them all, Liudmila the Ukrainian girl

that one September day, in Berlin
I ask her if her husband
of whom she spoke in the past tense

would be able to come to meet her soon,
with a break in her voice, she said to me
"Mein Mann... ist... vermisst."

"One day he left the house and then no one,
no one saw him any more.
For fourteen months, I have been waiting

for news, that we have been waiting, Klarina and I,
but she is so small, I don't believe
that she'll be able to remember".

Where now is Vilmante,
the lovely Lithuanian, and Arneta and the others?
Liudmila, wherever you are,

forgive me for putting you in a poem.

"Mein Mann ... ist ... vermisst" in German means: "My husband ... is ... missing."

Diario d'Irlanda

I

Farida, la ragazza sudanese
che non smette di ridere e protrae così la notte
rimandando a domani la iattura
dei compiti d'inglese,
ci chiede se crediamo nel malocchio,
poi si fa seria e spiega che da loro, a Khartum, le discariche
sono abitate dai genii, dagli spiriti:
«È meglio che tu preghi, se mai ci passi accanto;
temono solo l'acqua calda, i demoni,
e non è sempre detto che tu l'abbia
a portata di mano».
Di certo Farida non sa nulla
della feniletilamina di cui leggo
in questo libro sulla storia del cacao:
ce n'è nel cioccolato, vi si dice,
e ha benefici influssi sull'umore;
la sostanza è la stessa che il cervello
rilascia in varie dosi
quando ti adiri o quando ti innamori.
E se non lo sa Farida,
potrà saperlo la gazza che atterra
sul prato del cortile e se ne infischia del vento
che fa l'Irlanda più sola,
più isola?

Irish Diary

I

Farida, the Sudanese girl,
who can't stop laughing and so prolongs the night
leaving till to-morrow the catastrophe
of her English home work,
she asks us if we believe in the Evil Eye
then she turns serious, and explains that where she came
from, in Khartoum,
the rubbish dumps are filled with genies, with spirits:
"It's better to pray, if ever you pass nearby:
the demons are scared only of hot water
and, often, you don't have any with you."
Certainly, Farida knows nothing
about phenylalanine that I read
about in this book on the history of cocoa:
it is found in chocolate, so they say,
and it has good effects on the moods;
the substance is the same that the brain
releases in different amounts
when you get upset or are in love.
And if Farida doesn't know this,
will the magpie know this when it lands
on the lawn in the courtyard and doesn't give a damn for

the wind

that makes a more lonely Ireland,
more of an island?

II

Bayside è tranquilla stasera. Non piove più, qualcuno
porta a passeggio il cane, le cellule fotoelettriche
l'abbagliano nel punto che passa vicino alla porta qui accanto.
Dal lungomare stasera vedresti tutto il golfo, e Sandycove
e la collina di Dalkey con la brughiera di ginestre
dove ieri una coppia, seduta su massi pezzati di giallo lichene,
di spalle contro il cielo, come in un quadro di Friedrich,
contemplava la baia. Chi sapeva i nomi dei luoghi
con la mano spiegava il paesaggio, indicava
la sua casa lontana.

II

Bayside is quiet tonight. It has stopped raining, someone
is walking their dog, the automatic house-lights
dazzle him as he goes near next door.
From the Promenade this evening, you can see the whole bay,
                                        and Sandycove
and Dalkey hill with its gorse common
where yesterday, a couple, sat on rocks speckled with lichen
                                        yellow,
their backs to the sky, like a Friedrich painting,
and looked at the bay. Someone who knew the names of
                                        places,
pointed out the parts of the landscape, showed his house
in the distance.

This poem was written during De Marchi's visit to Dublin, Ireland, in 2002. The
nameplaces mentioned – Bayside (where Farida, the Sudanese student, was sharing a
flat with a friend of the poet), Sandycove and Dalkey – are along Dublin's coastline.

«In stranio suolo»

Un giorno d'aprile
una dama viennese
mi chiese cortese
se parlavo ungherese.

«No, parlo italiano,
ma anch'io son cortese,
mi dia la sua mano,
su, venga, balliamo».

The title is a quotation from *La traviata* (Act III, Scene IV), an opera by Francesco
Maria Piave (1810-1876) and Giuseppe Verdi (1813-1901).

"On foreign soil"

In Vienna on an April day
a courteous lady bade me stay
"I see you come from afar,
perhaps you even speak Magyar."

Swift I answered *piano piano*
"My only tongue is *italiano*.
but if you grant me your white hand,
we'll dance together on the strand."

Ninna nanna

Neanche per sogno
vuoi far la ninna
neanche se hai sonno
vuoi far la nanna:
ti mordi il pugno
ti graffi il naso
strofini il muso
contro la spalla
di chi ti canta
a ritmo di samba
la ninna nanna
finché non giunge
tra gli sbadigli
il formidabile
sonno dei bimbi
troppo più forte
della tua voglia
di stare sveglia.

Bye byes

No way
will you go bye byes
even if you are sleepy
you won't go bye byes:
you chew your fist
you scratch your nose
you nuzzle the shoulder
of someone singing you
bye byes
to a samba
until
the heavy sleep of babies
overcomes
the yawns
much stronger
than your will
to stay
awake.

Biciclette, generazioni

I

Il posto è quello adatto, il piazzale antistante la scuola
il tempo un pomeriggio di un giorno che non piove
gli attori padri e figlie con loro biciclette

la mia mano si stacca dal sellino e la bici
lanciata nella corsa non vacilla
no, non cadi, pedala, non avere paura

II

Mio padre tentò invano di insegnare
a suo padre ad andare in bicicletta, fu sul viale
della stazione di Greco-Pirelli

forse intanto passava un treno merci oppure il treno
che portava al paese di mia madre
a trovarla mio padre ci andava in bicicletta

III

Vedo il nonno Mariani, col cappello della domenica,
inforcare di slancio la sua bici da vedovo
attraversare il cortile fischiettando

andava a suonare ai vespri
solo negli ultimi anni si faceva accompagnare
in macchina da uno dei cantori

Bicycles, generations

I

The location is right, the small square in front of the school
the time, an afternoon of a day without rain,
the actors, fathers and sons with their bicycles.

my hand lets go of the saddle and the bike
thrust on its way does not waver
no, you won't fall off, keep pedaling, don't be scared

II

My father tried in vain to teach
his father how to ride a bicycle, it was in the lane
by the station at Greco-Pirelli

Perhaps, at the same time, a goods train went by or
perhaps it was the train to my mother's village,
to visit her there, my father always went by bike.

III

I saw grandpa Mariani, with his Sunday hat,
smoothly mounting his old lady's bike
to cross the courtyard whistling

he used to go to play for vespers
only in recent years he arranged to be taken by car
by someone in the choir

The Greco-Pirelli train station is in the northern suburbs of Milan.

Ancora verso Marina

Là dove l'altra estate fu un ramarro
la preda ignara di un giorno felice
pensi agli amori che durano più delle dune,
alla cicala che ricicla il suo canto,
tutti gli anni lo stesso.

Nel sole-ombra dei pini pare immune
dagli sgarbi del tempo
il tuo gusto feroce dell'estate.

Still towards Marina

There where on a good day last summer
a green lizard was an unwitting prey
you think of those loves who outlive the dunes,
of the cicada that recycles its song,
every year the same.

In the dappled light and shade of the pines,
your fierce relish for summer
seems immune to the insults of time.

For Marina di Grosseto and the green lizard see the note to 'Verso Marina' (p. 25).

Cena con geco, a Montepescali

Ha il colore ineffabile del tufo
il geco che sul muro apre di scatto
le micidiali mandibole, azzanna
la malcapitata falena e non gioca
come il gatto col topo,
la tiene immobile in bocca
per un minuto che pare infinito,
poi scappa via tra ciuffi di sassifraghe
lontano quanto basta
per masticarla in pace, al riparo
dagli sguardi indiscreti.

Dinner with a gecko, at Montepescali

It has the inexpressible colour of tufa
the gecko on the wall snaps
its murderous jaws, bites on
the unlucky butterfly; it doesn't
play like the cat with a mouse,
but holds it unmoving in its mouth
for an endless minute,
then it disappears in the tussock
far enough away
to chew in peace, away from
tactless glances.

Montepescali is a small medieval town near Grosseto, in Southern Tuscany, central Italy.

Come l'acqua

Quel giorno che qualcuno mi spiegò
che l'acqua trova sempre la sua strada
(le vasche del giardino disegnavano
un arduo labirinto)
cominciai a sognare d'essere acqua
anch'io: oh, traboccare, tracimare,
e come l'acqua andare verso il mare

Like water

The day when someone explained to me
that water always finds its own path
(the garden ponds laid out
an awkward labyrinth)
I began dreaming of being water,
myself: oh to spill over, to overflow,
and like water, to sea I'll go.

*FROM UNCOLLECTED AND
UNPUBLISHED POEMS (2007-2011)*

La vicina

Ha gli occhi rossi, la vicina, e dice
d'essersi accorta che lui stava male:
da giorni non sentiva il ticchettio
della macchina da scrivere.

Lei ci era abituata, a quel rumore:
«Ha scritto molto fino a poco tempo fa,
anche il suo stesso necrologio, ha detto Adele,
no, non il necrologio del giornale,

l'epitaffio, sì, insomma le parole
che metti sulla lapide.
L'ha fatto leggere ad Adele, e lei

gli ha detto: Mario, visto che ci sei,
scrivi anche il mio. E lui l'ha scritto. Poi
l'hanno portato lì, all'ospedale».

The neighbour

His neighbour has got red eyes, and says
she had noticed he was falling ill:
for days she didn't hear the tic-tic
of his typewriter.

She was used to it, to that noise:
"He wrote a lot until recently,
even his own obituary, Adele said,
no, not his obituary in the newspaper,

his epitaph, you know, those words
you put on the headstone.
He had Adele read it, and she

told him: Mario, now that you're at it,
write mine as well. And he wrote it. Then
they took him there, to the hospital."

Viaggiando verso il Monferrato

per Mimma e Giorgio

Lo dici commovente
il rosso dei papaveri nei fossi,
lungo le carreggiate dei sobborghi di Pavia,
ai bordi delle risaie allagate
o che «aspettano l'acqua».
Lo stesso vale, in pensiero,
per il blu dei fiordalisi,
che dei papaveri condividono le sorti
regressive: falcidiati da pesticidi, diserbanti,
si rifugiano ai margini dei campi,
tra i ruderi, o scompaiono alla vista.
E con loro, è l'estate
che smarrisce i suoi colori.

Travelling towards the Monferrato

for Mimma and Giorgio

You say it stirs you,
the red of poppies in the ditches,
along the lanes outside Pavia,
by the banks of rice fields flooded
or "waiting for water".
The same is true, if you think about it,
of the blue of corn flowers,
who share the same mortality
as the poppies: cut down by pesticides, weedkillers,
they hide in the edges of fields,
amidst ruins, or disappear out of sight.
And with them, it is summer's
colours that vanish.

The Monferrato is a large and mostly hilly territory in North-Western Italy,
stretching between Alessandria and Asti in Piedmont and Genova and Savona
in Liguria. Giorgio is the Swiss poet Giorgio Orelli (1921) and Mimma is his wife.
The city of Pavia, south of Milan, in North-Western Italy, was the capital of the
Longobard Kingdom in the Middle Ages and is the seat of one of Italy's and
Europe's oldest universities. The territory between Pavia and the Monferrato is one
rice field after another.

Nel paese delle fiabe

Nel recinto del vecchio cimitero
s'inseguono i bambini e le bambine, scavalcano
fiori secchi e granate tricolori
messe lì in piedi come granatieri,
fanno e rifanno un gaio girotondo
intorno al Monumento dei Caduti,
C'è n'è una, si chiama – ha detto – Alice,
sa le cose, le spiega agli altri, dice
che quelli sulle lapidi
«sono tutti pirati e capitani
che sono morti in guerra».

Il giorno dopo un'altra, e questa è Anita,
ripassando davanti al Monumento
dice che lei «non è più tanto giovane»
(l'altro ieri ha compiuto quattro anni!),
ma aggiunge, come per rassicurarmi,
che «i bambini non possono morire,
perché a morire sono solo i vecchi,
ma quelli proprio vecchi vecchi vecchi,
o quelli ch'erano tanto tempo fa,
o quelli che stanno lontano,
ma molto, molto lontano da qua».

In the land of the fairy tales

Inside the old cemetery
boys and girls chase each other, jump over
withered flowers and tricolour wreaths
placed there standing like grenadiers,
they keep gaily dancing round and round
the War Memorial.
One of them, her name is – she said – Alice,
she knows things, she explains them to the others, she says
that all the names on the headstones
"belong to pirates and captains
who died in war."

The day after another of them, this one called Anita,
going past the Memorial again
says that she's "no longer that young"
(the day before she turned four!),
but adds, as if to reassure me,
that "children cannot die,
because only the old die,
but only those really really old,
or those who lived a long time ago,
or those who live far,
very, very far away from here."

Rondò di Castelsardo

I gabbiani, dunque.
Per quanto tu resista
all'impulso di nominarli,
non c'è niente da fare:
è estate, tutto il giorno la finestra
è aperta e ad ora ad ora sopraggiungono
questi orgiastici gridi prolungati.

Ah, che vita da nababbo
ch'è quella del gabbiano:
nidifica sulle rocce a picco sul mare,
si fa portare dai venti,
che qui mai non restano,
e quando ha fame pesca
col becco non diritto ma neanche troppo adunco.

Castelsardo Rondo

Seagulls, then.
As much you resist
the impulse to mention them,
there's nothing to do:
it's summer, all day long the window
is open and from time to time those
prolonged orgiastic cries occur.

Ah, what a life of Reilly
the seagull leads:
he nests on sheer cliffs by the sea,
he lets himself be carried forth by the winds,
which never stop here,
and when he's hungry he fishes
with his beak, which is not straight but not too bent
either.

Castelsardo is a medieval seaside town near Sassari, in Sardinia, Italy.

La carta delle arance

e con ardente affetto il sole aspetta
Dante, *Par.*, XXIII 8

Quella carta velina, variopinta,
frusciante tra le dita
di chi la distendeva, la stirava con cura,
specie negli angoli, per innalzare
sotto i nostri occhi un fragile cilindro,
una precaria torre e poi incendiarla
con uno zolfanello, sulla cima;
e noi che aspettavamo intenti
di vederlo, quel sole di Sicilia
stampato sulla carta, sollevarsi
dal piatto con scrollo leggero
tramutantesi poi in volo tremulo –

ma più saliva più si consumava,
e, rimasto un istante sospeso nell'aria,
ecco un pezzo di sole annerito,
un frammento di torre in fiamme
ricadere sul piatto;
e allora, mentre ancora volteggiavano
sopra di noi coriandoli di carta strinata,
anche senza più fame
chiedevo un'altra arancia da sbucciare,
imploravo di rifarlo, ripeterlo,
quel gioco col fuoco.

Orange papers

e con ardente affetto il sole aspetta
Dante, *Par.*, XXIII 8

This tissue paper, multi-coloured,
rustling between the fingers
that smoothed it, stretched it carefully,
especially at the corners, to erect
before our eyes a fragile cylinder,
a flimsy tower and then to light it
at its summit, with a match;
and we who had waited intently
to see it, this sun of Sicily
printed on the paper, lifting off
the dish with a slight shrug,
then turning into trembling flight –

but the higher it went, the more it burned,
and, remaining an instant suspended in the air,
look a piece of burnt up sun
a fragment of the flaming tower
falls back on the ground:
and then, while this confetti of scorched paper
still floated about us,
and even though no longer hungry
I kept on asking for another orange to peel,
I was begging to do it again, to have another go,
this playing with fire.

In Allen Mandelbaum's translation (*The Divine Comedy of Dante Alighieri: Paradiso*, 1984), the quotation reads as: "as she awaits the sun with warm affection."

Madrigale per A.

When we moved I had your measure and you had mine
—Seamus Heaney, 'Tate's Avenue'

E poi il tornante dove abbandonarono
il Maggiolino Volkswagen celeste,
la radura nel bosco dove videro

la luna farsi sempre più tonda, meno rossa
nel cielo ad ogni istante più blu,
blu notte d'agosto,

e alla fine il corteo dei borghigiani,
con le torce e coi cani,
tutti accorsi a cercare i padroni

del Maggiolino Volkswagen celeste,
per paura che fossero caduti
nel dirupo, o si fossero perduti.

Madrigal for A.

When we moved I had your measure and you had mine
— Seamus Heaney, 'Tate's Avenue'

And then the hairpin bend where they left
the blue Volkswagen Beetle,
the wood's clearing where they saw

the moon become rounder and rounder, less red
in the sky bluer with every moment passing,
August midnight blue,

and in the end the parade of villagers
with flashlights and dogs,
all gathered to look for the owners

of the blue Volkswagen Beetle,
for fear that they had fallen
down the steep slope, or were lost.

The quotation is from a love poem titled after the name of a street in Belfast,
Northern Ireland, where Heaney lived, studied and worked before moving to
Dublin, in the Republic of Ireland.

Momento di tregua

I

Il mostro è qui, la ruspa dalle chele d'acciaio,
dirocca i muri toccandoli appena,
si sposta provocando il maggior crollo
con il minimo sforzo.

Ora la casa è sventrata, a sezione verticale.
Niente a che vedere con *La vie
mode d'emploi*, eppure anche qui
chi osserva dai balconi circostanti

indovina la forma delle stanze,
gli aloni sugli intonaci, l'intreccio
dei tubi dove l'acqua come il sangue
in un corpo saliva e discendeva…

II

È un momento di tregua, la pausa delle nove.
Un vecchio, un uomo giovane, una donna,
tre bambini (chi sono?) vanno e vengono,

mettono in salvo gli infissi, le imposte,
il legno ancora buono. Torneranno
tra poco gli operai dai caschi gialli,

Moment of truce

I

The monster is here, the excavator with steel claws,
crumbling walls just by touching them,
and as it moves causing the most damage
with the least effort.

Now the house is gutted vertically.
Nothing to do with *La vie
mode d'emploi*, yet here too
those who look on from nearby balconies

can figure out the shape of the rooms,
the marks on the plaster, the network
of pipes where water was rising and falling
like blood in a body …

II

It's a moment of truce, the nine o'clock pause.
An old man, a young man, a woman,
three children (who are they?) come and go,

they rescue frames, shutters,
the wood that's still good. The workers
with yellow helmets will come back soon,

s'aggireranno nel cortile controllando
lo stato dei lavori. Demolito quanto resta,
comincerà lo scavo.

they'll walk around the yard to check
the work in progress. Once what's left is demolished,
they'll begin digging.

La vie mode d'emploi (1978) is a novel by the French novelist, filmmaker,
documentalist and essayist, Georges Perec (1936-1982).

Lettera da Zurigo

Mentre qui fuori i merli
s'avventano sull'albero di sorbo
che allunga i rami a sfiorare il sambuco
e con avidità ne inghiottono le bacche scarlatte
prima di volar via, spaventati da un'ombra,
mi viene in mente che volevo scriverti;
perché l'ultima volta che t'ho visto
m'hai snocciolato una serie di nomi di uccelli
in dialetto, tra cui i *finchi*, fringuelli
in italiano, *Finken* in tedesco,
ed io non ho potuto non pensare a Pascoli,
che tu forse non avevi mai letto.
Ma non importa: finché campo, con o senza merli
nei dintorni di sorbi o di sambuchi,
mi ricorderò di te, e dei *finchi*
e dell'ultima volta che t'ho visto.

Letter from Zurich

While out here blackbirds
rush to the rowan
whose branches touch the elder
and they greedily eat the scarlet berries
before flying off, scared away by a shadow,
I remember I wanted to write to you;
because the last time I saw you
you reeled off in dialect one bird's name
after another, including *finchi*, finches
in Italian, *Finken* in German,
and I couldn't help thinking of Pascoli,
whom you've never read perhaps.
But it's not important: as long as I live, with
or without blackbirds near rowans or elders,
I will remember you, and the *finchi*,
and the last time I saw you.

The poet alludes to 'Il fringuello cieco' ('The Blind Finch', 1903), a poem by the
Italian poet Giovanni Pascoli (1855-1912).

Di un cavallo e di un carro

Come falso veder bestia quand'ombra
— Dante, *Inf.*, II 48

Al suo cavallo baio
dalle poderose culatte
e dalla coda a frusta
terrore delle mosche vespertine
il mugnaio Calistro
poneva sulle tempie
neri paraocchi di cuoio
perché a quell'ora il suo ruolo
era tirare il carro
stracarico di sacchi di farina
bianca o gialla, per pane o per polenta,
non distrarsi a guardare
chi lo faceva adombrare:
noi, ad esempio, pronti a saltare
a cavalcioni sui sacchi
per farci portare a zonzo
come cow-boy dell'Arizona o dell'Ohio,
almeno fino a quando
terminate le consegne
il mugnaio emetteva l'ultimo "arri"
e noi si saltava giù in corsa
prima che lui s'arrabbiasse
per finta o per davvero.

Of a horse and a cart

Come falso veder bestia quand'ombra
—Dante, *Inf.*, II 48

On his horse, reddish brown
with a massive rump
and a tail that scares off
the evening flies,
Calistro the miller
put black leather blinkers
because at that time of day
the horse
had to pull the cart
heavy laden with flour sacks
white or yellow, for bread or polenta,
and was not to be distracted
by those who would make him shy.
We, for example, were always ready
to jump on and straddle the sacks
to ride around heedlessly
like cowboys in Arizona or Ohio,
at least until the miller,
finished with his deliveries,
cried the last "whoa!"
and we jumped down and ran away
before he got angry
or maybe he just pretended to be angry.

In Allen Mandelbaum's translation (*The Divine Comedy of Dante Alighieri: Inferno*, 1980), the quotation reads as: "as phantoms frighten beasts when shadows fall."

Lullaby

per Michel Petrucciani

Ritmi di vita che pulsa
di vita che sfida la morte
sì, ritmi di vita che pulsa che sfida
la morte

l'amore la vita
lullaby, sillabe, oh sì
oh no, oh nana
oye

vorrei saper scrivere come tu suoni, vorrei
lasciar dire alle dita

Lullaby

for Michel Petrucciani

Rhythms of life that beats
of a life that challenges death
yeah, rhythms of life that beats that challenges
death

love life
lullaby, syllables, oh yeah
oh no, oh nana
oye

I would like to be able to write as you play, I would like
to let my fingers speak

The title of the poem is the title of a piece by the French jazz pianist Michel
Petrucciani (1962-1999).

Il disincanto e la metrica

> *Now after so many years the other voice*
> *doesn't remember it and maybe believes I'm dead.*
> — Eugenio Montale, 'Late at night'

A Heathrow, all'aeroporto,
per ingannare l'attesa
leggo Montale tradotto in inglese,
e mi ritorna in mente l'altra estate

quando mio padre al telefono ha chiesto
se era arrivata posta,
ma non cose per lui senza importanza,
bollette della luce o resoconti della banca.

«Cartoline, per caso?»
«Mi dispiace», dicevo, »non c'è niente»,
e allora ha pronunciato quella frase

che adesso mi ridico senza sosta
(«si vede che mi credono già morto»),
perfetto endecasillabo di sesta.

The quotation from Montale's 'A tarda notte' (1968) is in Harry Thomas'
translation (*Literary Imagination*, 2:3, 2000).

Disenchantment and prosody

Ormai dopo tanti anni l'altra voce
non lo rammenta e forse mi crede morto.
    — Eugenio Montale, 'A tarda notte'

At Heathrow, at the airport,
to kill time
I read Montale in English translation,
and last summer comes to mind

when my father asked me over the phone
if there had been any mail,
and not things of no importance to him,
power bills or bank statements, but:

"Postcards, by any chance?"
"I'm sorry," I told him, "nothing,"
and then he uttered that sentence,

that now I repeat to myself all the time
("obviously they think I'm already dead,")
a perfect hendecasyllable.

Luna crescente, stella filante

Tutto accade così in fretta, e la luna
crescente che stampava sulla roccia rossastra,
verticale, le nostre silhouette affiancate
inarrestabilmente ora tramonta,
si fa minuscola, è un punto di luce,
una biglia di buio
che esplode.
         Non la vale
la miriade d'astri della notte d'agosto,
né quell'unica stella filante
che insieme abbiamo visto attraversare
un lungo tratto di cielo, fulminea, più rapida
del desiderio in cerca di parole.

Crescent moon, shooting star

Everything happens so quickly, and the crescent
moon that was printing on red rock,
vertically, our side-by-side silhouettes
is inexorably going down,
is becoming small, it's a dot of light,
an exploding billiard ball
of darkness.
         The myriad
of stars in the August night can't match it,
not even that single shooting star
that we saw together as it crossed
a long stretch of sky, like lightning, faster
than giving words to a wish.

APPENDIX

Augenlicht

… miro este querido mundo
que se deforma y que se apaga
en una pálida ceniza vaga …
    – J.L. Borges, Poema de los dones

I

È come stare dentro a un videogame,
e tu sei l'orso, il grizzly che prendono di mira;
a ogni colpo del laser che rattoppa,
un lampo verde, una fitta sottile.
Il microscopio fruga, mette a fuoco
la retina strappata e tu contempli
una landa lunare, una pianura tutta crepe:
puoi pensare, se vuoi, alle crete di Burri.

II

"L'occhio è un organo chiuso, ma keine Angst,
la lieve emorragia dovrebbe riassorbirsi."
Non si riassorbe, invece, ed ecco allora
cavallucci marini, ombre cinesi,
volatili figure nere e strane.
Mouches volantes? Macché,
piuttosto grossi corvi con le ali spiegate.
Tecnicamente, eine massive Blutung.

III

Una tenace pece
bluastra e gialla ingromma il cristallino:

Augenlicht

… miro este querido mundo
que se deforma y que se apaga
en una pálida ceniza vaga …
        – J.L. Borges, Poema de los dones

I

It's like being inside a videogame,
and you're the bear, the targeted grizzly;
at every laser shot to patch up your eye,
a green lightning, a subtle pang,
the microscope searches, zooms in
on the torn retina and you gaze on
a lunar land, a valley full of cracks:
you can think, if you like, of Burri's crettos.

II

"The eye is a closed organ, but keine Angst,
the slight bleeding will be reabsorbed.
Except that it's not reabsorbed and so
water horses, shadow plays,
black and strange flying creatures.
Mouches volantes? Not in the least;
instead, large crows with wings outstretched.
Technically, eine massive Blutung.

III

A tenacious tar
bluish and yellow gums up the crystalline:

se muovi il capo, se giri lo sguardo
tutto nell'occhio si mette a frullare
ed una parte del mondo s'invola.
Quando appare una nuvola
nerissima, sfrangiata,
e sotto, lungo l'orlo,
vedi lampi che corrono
per linee orizzontali,
non c'è tempo da perdere,
ora tocca al chirurgo.

IV

Con grazia l'Augenschwester
ti libera la guancia dai cerotti, solleva
anche il guscio di plastica, la garza, dischiude
le ciglia ingombre di pomata e sangue: meravigliosamente
tutto riprende il suo posto, il soffitto,
la finestra, le case, le colline
là dietro l'alta torre che s'arrampica
al cielo, a Züri West.

if you move your head, if you look around
everything in the eye starts whirring
and a part of the world takes flight.
When a cloud appears,
very black, frayed,
and underneath it, along the edge,
you see lightning running
horizontally,
there's no time to waste,
now it's up to the surgeon.

IV

Gracefully the Augenschwester
removes the plasters from your cheek, lifts
also the plastic guard, the gauze, slightly opens
the eyelashes glued up with ointment and blood: everything
wonderfully returns to its place, the ceiling,
the window, the houses, the hills
over there behind the tall tower climbing
to the sky, in Züri West.

The epigraph in Spanish are the first three lines from the last quatrain of Jorge Luis
Borges' 'Poema de los dones' (El Hacedor, 9 August 1960). Borges was going blind when
he wrote this poem after being nominated Director of the National Library of Argentina
in Buenos Aires. In Victoria Ríos Castano's English translation the epigraph reads: "I
look at this beloved world / that deforms and extinguishes / into pale and vague ashes."
In German "Augenlicht" means "eyesight". Alberto Burri (1915-1995) was an Italian
abstract painter and sculptor. Burri worked with unorthodox materials and made collages
with pumice, tar, and burlap, creating a series of tri-dimensional canvases. In the early
1970s he began his so-called "cracked" paintings, or cretti. In German "keine Angst"
means "don't worry". In French "mouches volants" (from the Latin muscae volitantes, or
"flying flies") means "floaters". Floaters are deposits within the eye's vitreous humour. The
common type of floater (present in most people's eyes) is due to degenerative changes of
the vitreous humour. They may appear as spots, threads, or fragments of cobwebs, which
float slowly before your eyes. In German "eine massive Blutung" means "a severe haemor-
rhage" and an "Augenschwester" is an ophthalmological nurse. Züri West is a developing
trendy suburb of Zurich.

About the Author/Translator

Pietro De Marchi (Seregno, 1958) is a *Titularprofessor* of Italian at the University of Zurich and a *Professeur associé* at the University of Neuchâtel, where he lectures in Comparative Literature. He also teaches at the University of Bern. A widely published critic and editor of scholarly editions, he is an award winning poet.

Marco Sonzogni is an academic and translator living in New Zealand.

Printed in September 2012
by Gauvin Press,
Gatineau, Québec